Liminal Existing

a poetry collection

Ren Ashe

India | USA | UK

Made with ❤ on the BookLeaf Publishing Platform
www.bookleafpub.in
www.bookleafpub.com

Dedication

To Aaron:
You are my best friend, my partner, my favorite human.
I never could have done this without your support.
I love you forever and always.

To my kids:
No one has taught me more about myself and about life
than you two have.
I love you both more than I could ever properly describe.

Preface

I never really seriously considered releasing a poetry collection, but not because I hadn't written any. In fact, poetry has been a go-to genre of mine for pretty much as long as I've been writing. But it has also felt incredibly personal, more so than other genres such as fiction or essays, which is where the rest of my writing focus has generally fallen.

As someone who feels incredibly protective of my writing (purely from a place of trying to spare myself embarrassment), the idea of this rawest form of writing being the one I chose to go 'public' with was... overwhelming, at times.

However, my resolve to see it through came in two main forms:

1. The desire to feel like I finally lived up to my potential in some way (rise up, my fellow burnt out former gifted kids), and

2. I'd spent my entire conscious life shrinking myself down and making myself more digestible, for fear of being too much or too upfront for others, and this was a very decided step in a new direction.

Acknowledgements

A sincere thank you and acknowledgement to my partner and best friend, Aaron, for reminding me of my worth, for pushing me to write this book, and for working to facilitate everything I needed for this book to actually happen.

dead name

I usually say 'birth name' instead.

'Government name' if I feel cheeky.

Because it isn't really a *dead* name.

If it is, then I must be dragging a partial corpse behind me, a grayed and weathered cadaver of a prefix.

Or did the name fully die, and I simply resurrected just a part of it, selectively deeming the backend of the horse to be the winner of the costume contest?

Did I coax it back to this side of the veil through a gender affirming Ouija board session? Did the planchette dance out those letters for me? Do I tell myself this to justify my asking to be haunted?

Clinging to the battered half zombie moniker like a child clings to their security blanket, not allowing myself a full rebirth, only this stunted half death, this abrupt splicing of myself, as if I could simply cut away the *before*, as if any of this were as simple as nomenclature.

cycle

Maybe they read too much into it.
Maybe it isn't all that bad.
Maybe downplaying this is the riskiest thing they could
do outside of being a *they* in the bible belt.

Some days, their esophagus seems intent on simulating
roller coaster level jitters
*(Imagine: The sharp turns, the sudden drops, the
deafening in your ears, the full visceral response),*
when the most they've done is
sign for a package,
waited for a text,
missed a line of their to-do list.

Their leg finds its usual bouncing rhythm,
the motion churning out a lulling melody to which their
anxiety can really dance.
*(Listen: The tempo incessantly unpredictable and jarring,
like freeform jazz Live from the Limbic System)*
The rubber on their heel must be getting low, the tread
slowly fading as deep tracks give way to low valleys
which soon become a barren plain of numb
forgetfulness.
Forgetfulness as in

*When did this even start? Was this rubber ever so fully
formed? Did it not come this way?*
They can now smell the rubber, it actively burning away
from friction as their heel grinds out the beat of their
own internal screaming.
Internal screaming as in
*Who flickers these gaslights anyway? Someone must be
in the house, and they must be here to get me.*
But of course, they are they.

The fabricating fuels their illness and their illness fuels
the fabricating and if that isn't the most fatally tragic
cycle then who knows where to begin.
Where to begin as in
When did this even start?

self care

I swear, my anxiety could burn a hole in my stomach
faster than any late night order of the number four
combo
(Yeah sure, I'll upgrade to a large)
ever could.
Do they make Tums for minds that churn in excess? Or
is that just Delta 8?
A trendy mental illness is like finally feeling understood
while simultaneously feeling invalidated and unworthy
of addressing your own issues, which were there piling
up on the floor long before TikTok became the new
diagnostic tool
(Cue Alanis Morissette in three, two, one).
I avoid social media.
I learn my triggers, my risk factors, my must-do habits,
my avoid-these-actions, my *please-just-do-this-and-
maybe-it'll-stop* routine.
I follow daily rituals, self care myself into submission, all
to appease the Trinity that guides my life:
In the name of the
Anxiety, the
Depression, and the
BPD.
Ah, fuck.

this one rhymes

One day I'll be naught but bones and dust,
my flesh will weaken and my mind will rust.
In years to come my image shall fade,
my body stagnant, my brain decayed.
This final chapter I fear not,
when skin has withered and muscles rot.
I'll see no angels, no pearly gates,
and nor do I wish for such a fate.
Instead I shall return to be
threads of the universe, the purest me.

autopsy of an adolescent summer

The collective body appears youthful, taut, fresh.

Raw, naive, vulnerable.

Unassuming.

Ideal.

Skin is chlorine marinated and UV baked, grit of sweat beads long evaporated in the sunset breeze dapple the surface like the sparsest sandpaper.

Scalpel coaxes flesh open like a lover's sweet words coax lips to part and, in similar baffled and churning passion, out pour forth the innards, all confused and hyperbolized distress. Roiling self loathing has ravaged so much of the tissue that had once dried tears and fought fears but now seems to just fester, a smoldering rot too worthless even to fully die.

Extracted and weighed, the scale reads out the full heft of the existence of this mass: tugging at eyelids, scratching at flesh, all to release an itch that was never even there; three point seven kilograms of guilt and self hatred.

The rest has already spilt out onto the floor, the autopsy table overrun with just how much had been kept bottled up inside. A bloated corpse gorged on denial and downplay, now professing itself in this grotesque

confessional, all of its skeletons traipsing one by one
from the closet to *danse macabre* to the rhythm of this
visceral elegy, this witness to barest truths and purest
fears.

The organs present themselves: an array of cured meats,
aged and brined for years, the salt of lessons learned and
of curses muttered crusting over the edges and sides.

The heart

is achy, tender, raw; far too swollen with childish naivete
and far too removed from reality to admit it.

The lungs

are lined with too many held breaths left for too long to
fester and putrefy into near drowning. Etchings of scar
tissue give evidence to the damage, panicked scrawling
counting down the days, weeks, months, years.

The stomach

is full to bursting with bitten off words and choked down
pain, the oldest of these hardened into a bezoar of self
sabotage. The pit in the stomach: not a hole, but a stone,
the flesh long torn away and sucked dry, leaving nothing
but a heavy weight, a sinking mass. The hypothetical life
within straining to find purchase in this acid field where
things only break down, never grow.

The brain

is bruised and achy from confronting countless walls in
senseless demands for silence, for serenity, for eternal
sunshine and spotlessness.

balance

Your strong hands keep me grounded
but never buried.
Your warm arms keep me safe
but never caged.
Your voice of reason guides me
but never commands.
Your very presence comforts me
but never controls me.

You steady my racing mind.
Thoughts go from blurred spiral to discernible shapes,
colors, ideas.
You calm my turbulent heart.
Emotions once tossed on an unsettled ocean now find
refuge in your patience.
You balance my teetering spirit.
Amidst the sprinting from one end to the other, I see you
waiting for me in the gray middle ground
I often forget exists.

lines of power

Blood runs like sap, sticky
and lingering,
while roots reach out tendrils desperately seeking
nature, nurture, nutrients.
Arms reach up, grasping at potential, at growth, at
progress.
Pull cord powered petroleum smoke chokes the air and
branches fall, lifeless and without reach.
Because they got too close to the lines of power.
They made themselves a threat, by trying to reach the
sunshine,
by trying to live.

dammed

There are spaces and cracks where the real me leaks out from time to time.

First, just little pores in the otherwise pristine and meticulous repair work, a small weak spot, a vulnerability left unchecked in the filled-in gaps left behind by others and their self servicing.

Later, blatant fractures worn to gaping wounds in the shoddily thrown together repair job, the time and care for meticulous work long lost to the exhaustion of constant constructions and reconstruction.

My mask is a cracked dam near to bursting, the unassuming village of my life blissfully unaware of the deluge's imminence.

And what if the dam breaks?

What happens if I flood my life with my truest self?

What if the entire village gets washed away until there is nothing left to even indicate that it had ever been there at all?

Was I the village, or am I the flood?

anxiety, an acrostic

A is for always over analyzing anything the appears at all off or absurd. Actively assessing any possible accident or aggravation. Always avoiding answering (the door, the phone, self reflective questions). Absorbing myself absolutely in Animal Crossing. Adding anything that appropriates adolescence and that all together more amiable area of existing. Admiring adults who apparently achieve all their activities without aid from antidepressants. Arguing against my own personal advocate of the Devil to attempt to assuage my ample amount of agonizing guilt.

N is for not now, it's too much.

water

I am water.
Unbound, wild, unyielding.
All I know is how to spread myself thin.
I give all of myself into whatever I'm placed.
I am necessary, needed, thirsted after.
I see myself as just a puddle, commonplace and mundane.
I see others, the wine with its sensual deep red hue.
I don't make people feel good like wine does, its sexy drops consuming their senses as deeply as they consume it.
I wish I could be wine: sexy, confident, knowing I am wanted.
But I am just water.

And you... the water bearer. You collect me, protect me.
You've never contained me or controlled me; you've kept me secure.
You've replenished me when I let myself slosh out onto the floor.
You guard me and guide me, tell me how much I quench your thirst.
You tell me how wine can be fun, but it's fleeting.
You tell me how, without water, life is empty.

I am water.

I am all that I reflect, and as you gaze into me
I am love.

membership: denied

I didn't ask for your sacrifice,

sacrament,

sacred words.

Your sanctuary offers no solace.

The sin that spills from my soul has definitely sealed my

fate, a no admittance sign hastily splattered across the

gates, the still wet paint staining a dusk laden sky.

I've never cared for clubs you buy your way into

anyway.

resilience is not a compliment.

Do not expect me to thank you for gifting me resilience.
Do not expect me to greet the flesh aching memories
with grace.
Do not expect me to express forgiveness in the name of
'self care' or 'inner peace.'
Resilience is not a compliment, much like how silence is
not consent.
A wild animal that doesn't thrash against the bars of a
cage isn't welcoming forced captivity:
It's *frightened.*
Fight or flight is a misnomer,
and freezing can happen even in a Georgia July heat.

why are they called blades of grass?

Flesh pressed against the musty earth, moss smothered rocks, loamy soil.

'Why are they called blades of grass?'

The green carpet seemed to be capable of only caressing and cushioning their bodies, not of slaughtering them and leaving their blood to seep deeply into the earth, the dirt itself seeming to feel a ravenous thirst given the eagerness with which the life essence is so utterly consumed and taken under.

'These shouldn't be called blades.'

Blades are steel and iron, manmade and harsh. Blades are for cutting, slicing, stabbing, gutting, hacking, eviscerating, severing, executing. Blades are what come soaring down from the pinnacle of the guillotine. Blades are what get pressed to a man's throat for saying the wrong thing to the wrong person.

Blades are what ring out in clashing glory in battle.

'Something so docile should not bear such a violent name.'

The grass is gentle, soft, lulling, enticing, enchanting. No painful tearing of metal through flesh, no violence at all. Just growth. Just expansion. Just existence.

Blades command attention, whether in the shimmer of

their hilt, the razor sharpness of their edge, or the threatening glare of the sunlight off their polished surface.

'But grass is so subtle, yet ever so present without even trying.'

Flesh pressed into earth, individual knives of grass weave silently, subtly, between flesh and bone, between muscle and skin. Green claws dig their way through, in, out, around, and in between, eyes rolling as tendrils of optic and vegetation tangle and fight for space just behind the curtain. Bones crunch like so many crisp autumn leaves underfoot. Jaw hangs loose as a deluging arsenal of grass floods from and into the distorted orifice that may have once resembled a mouth but now seems to be little more than a tattered panel of skin, left to mother nature's devices.

allow me to alliterate

Listen to this language of languid languishing and of
relinquishing one's reliquary of relics and legends.
The legerdemain of legacy is lengthy and often
loathsome, those elongated and elocutionary cautionary
Canterbury tales, can't really tell how to make heads or
tails.
So instead try to tell these twisted tales traipsing to
topple from the tip of the tongue, these words watered
down and weak from weeks wasted on waiting for one
obvious occurrence of optimal, or even obtuse, passion to
come towards me.
Come, passion, towards me.
Compassion towards me, towards myself, comes
crushingly in coarsely chopped chunks, calling to mind
something that would be closer kin to
callous,
careless,
cared less for,
less than others,
left behind,
lead in my legs as I am dragging my begrudging and
belligerent bellyaching,
belaying the betrayal of my own behavior to the brink
before being blindly brandished into the blackness

beyond.

Words have a wizened yet wiry way of wandering, woefully or wonderfully, betwixt the windows and wormholes of my well-worn shirt sleeve, where I shelve my slumbering slab of cardiac sinew, it slogging the Sisyphean span of its skills while simultaneously spooning out sensations, both surreptitious and sonorous as well as some sum settled somewhere in the sands between the silent and the screaming.

Every imaginable effect and emotion, each energy shift and every anticipatory elevation of expectation, each of these eases into its own existence and engineered chaos, causing cacophonous crowing of the coming of a calamitous and cataclysmic reckoning sure to render all reason beyond recognition as the rolling rhythm rumbles like thunder through the trees at the triumph of summertime, the tingle of electric threads in the thick atmosphere.

'So sensitive' slips like smoothest silk from such sour pouts, putting on perfect pedestal presentation the precise petulance and petty preferences that proceed to be proudly professed from the practiced pair of porcelain postures.

So fragile flashes fluidly in the forefront of my thoughts, *fragile* as the facade falls free from its former function, the falsehoods forming its framework failing to find footing in its frail and fraught foundation.

low hanging fruit

Overripe from too many days forgotten in the sun,
others' indifference towards me swelling my flesh like a
corpse left to rot in the sludge and weeds of a brackish
pond.
Too eager, my skin cracks and gives way at the slightest
pressure, the slightest indication of want.
I can't hold myself together, the seams have all burst and
the dam has broken and all of me has come undone.
I seep into the soil, my rot unspooling itself into the
earth, all to be regrown, reformed, reborn.
A human ouroboros, I contain my own ending.
A tragic emotional phoenix, I rise only to fail again.

siren song

Lighthouse keeper, shine your halogen guidance this way.
The sea is still but deceit lies just below the surface.
Inky black undulations gently sway me, lulling me to and fro. Your light glares past me, the shadows cloaking the sinister salinity with an even heavier wash of deepest cerulean.
Perhaps I can do this alone.
It does not seem too harrowing.
I even hear beautiful singing.

immortal lovers

Your hands fit my body so well, as if it'd been you who had hewn my flesh into being, molding and caressing me into existence, leaving traces of gaps only you could fill, silent etchings in my soul that can only feel alive when you are near.
My soul sails in your veins, my body jealous of this closeness.
I picture my hands, already pressed firmly against your skin,
imagine them sinking in deeper,
slowly,
gently.
I imagine the closeness of crawling inside of your flesh, of taking up roost in your bones, housing my heart beside yours, feeling ourselves forever enmeshed, unable to ever be fully separate or apart, an eternal 'us' dripping, flowing, coalescing forevermore together, until we are everything and nothing at once.
Once we've fed the forests,
nourished the animals,
and been spread to the sky, we will be deeper entwined into continual life.
We'll be immortal lovers, parts of us in every thing, until

we've seen the entire universe and everything is star
dust once more.

ritual

No safety net, I lurch forward in a fully unrecognizable arc well beyond the conditional confines of the oral tradition.

The only hands to reach me here are just capable of being dragged down, even as they reach as eager as those who could actually help, yearning so earnestly to save me that they succeed in only sacrificing themselves.

It isn't sacrifice if they don't realize.

Not of the 'self' variety, anyway.

I never asked to perform this ritual, but the blade finds itself at home in my palm just the same.

sleep suspended

It feels like waking up,
like a heavy coat of hibernation has been lifted away
after housing all its tucked away inhabitants for
years and years that have blurred into one another as a
mottled and swirled galaxy,
whose twinkling stars have only just begun to reflect in
my eyes, as if seeing them for
the first time.

plot twist

There is no storyline to follow here.
No clear path to tread, its surface well packed by all the previous travelers' burdened feet.
No flash of neon splashed across the bark of the ancient guards around us to denote a direction.
Uncharted territory springs to mind, but the term feels meaningless and hollow.
Another victim to the sentencing that is incessant repetitive use, each recitation stripping away more and more of its meaning, the varnish of its contextual significance fading with every repetition, until it remains little more than a noise, an utterance that hints at some sort of meaning, yet your brain refuses to grant it purchase, and it slips effortlessly down the well-worn gulleys and paths carved by all those constant refrains of the words which now linger as mere ghosts of their former selves.
And so you find yourself lost in the woods on a snowy evening, craving sleep but we know how that goes.
The wind is biting, all fangs and froth, and the chill is harsh enough to burn. Your skin feels every clamp of the jaws, and your flesh sears as the elements pay you in exposure.
Giving in to these hungry dogs feels almost hopeful, as if

this could be the very thing you were in these woods to
find in the first place: *Release.*
Release the hounds onto yourself, you self-scorning
Jezebel. No windows to fall from in the woods at night,
but these dogs will feast upon your very soul just the
same.
Letting the elements take you back into themselves
seems far preferable to admitting that this was
no simple sojourn, that you
should not have journeyed solo.
Sitting so low in your stomach as a lump of spoiled food
that spreads its sickness throughout your body like
tendrils of blood spreading through water,
the idea of *just letting go* settles into your mind with a
sickening thud,
like the sound of your toe crashing into a table leg; even
the weird sense of nausea is the same, catching your
tongue in your throat like your own body is revolted by
itself.
Surrendering to the scenery wouldn't be so bad, now
would it?
To lay down to rest in the frosted landscape knowing
you would never wake again.
To let the cold into your bones and let the breath out of
your lungs.
To worship face down in the clearest pool of the iciest
waters.

To feel the cold and the chill and the exhaustion just
melt away until the darkness welcomes you home.
Eyes closed, you're ready for the darkness to come.
The chill has lost its edge, the wind's bite is all gums and
bark.
This must be it, you think. *Release.*
You can almost hear it coming on now.
The strange, melodic, welcoming call of...
Birdsong. Spring's return.
The wheel has kept turning, as it always does.
The sun shines earlier, the days feel warmer, your eyes
see sharper,
and you realize that *uncharted territory* holds no
meaning here because,
somehow, for once, you know *exactly*
where you are.

vessel

This vessel of mine has played both prison and paradise.
I've dressed and draped my altar in fineries, then left the
temple trashed the next morning.
Tossed it about like I always knew it would bounce back,
or else that I didn't give a shit if it did or not.
I was meant to loathe this backhanded gift horse while
fully shoving my head inside of its mouth, never
bothering to notice this oven of an orifice. Now the gas
line is open and my vision is underwater and my ears are
stuffed with cotton and my lungs are full of fire and--
No more.
I reject your prescribed hatred, your requisite loathing,
your compulsory self disgust, all of it coalescing into this
bizarre ritual of eating away at myself in some emotional
emulation of autocannibalism.
This flesh of mine will feel grass and warm embraces.
This skin of mine will be kissed by the sun and by lovers'
lips.
This vessel of mine will *live.*

www.ingramcontent.com/pod-product-compliance
Lightning Source LLC
La Vergne TN
LVHW010951200726
843509LV00013B/2365